Techatticup Mine

Jane Moorman

I love exploring areas off the main highways. You never know what you will find.

A friend once said, "I wish I could see the world as Jane sees it. Finding the beauty in things that most of us don't take time to see."

While driving to Las Vegas, Nevada, I took a road that led to the Colorado River and discovered this restored mining town. It was so full of interesting things that I just had to stop. This book contains what I found.

Jane Moorman, photographer

Mining Days Gone By

South of Las Vegas, Nevada, on US 95 a sign stating Nelson with an arrow pointing toward the Colorado River caught my eye. As I turned towards Nelson, 10 miles on a paved road, another sign saying Eldorado Canyon 18 miles, sounded interesting. The adventure began as I drove east toward the canyon on a winding road.

Now referred to as the town of Nelson, this area was originally called El Dorado in 1775 by Spaniards who uncovered gold in the area. In the mid-1880s when prospectors and miners flooded the western United States, they completely inundated the canyon.

In 1857, steamboat entrepreneur Captain George Alonzo Johnson re-established the area's name as Eldorado Canyon. The canyon drains into the Colorado River at the former site of Nelson's Landing. The location of the mines was ideal with access to the navigable river, making it possible to bring food and supplies to the miners, as well as additional prospectors.

The road through the canyon ends at the river. Halfway through the canyon the remains of Techatticup Mine are on both sides of the road. Techatticup Mine was the largest and most productive mine in the Colorado Mining District. The camps of Alturas and Louisville were located near by.

Techatticup Mine is one of the areas discovered by the Spaniards. The 1880s prospectors took over the already established mine. Some of the first prospectors were deserters of the Civil War. Both former Union and Confederate soldiers set up camp here, assuming such an isolated location would be the last place military authorities would search for them.

With an estimated 500 miners in the area, it was a bustling, rough-and-tumble township Shootouts and murders were so frequent during the 1880s that they were an assumed part of ordinary life. Despite the lawlessness, the area was one of the largest booms the state of Nevada ever encountered.

Producing gold, silver, copper, and lead, the Techatticup, Wall Street and Savage mines wielded $5 million dollars during the 40 years of operation.

Flash floods in the area are common and in 1974 disaster struck. With a wall of water and debris towering at nearly 40 feet, nine people were killed and much of the village was destroyed.

In 1994, Tony and Bobbie Werly bought the property from the company that had owned the mine since 1929. During the next 20-plus years, the Werly family restored the buildings that were abandoned after the 1974 flood.

Anything that could be removed from the property, such as doors and equipment, had been taken by scavengers. All the cars and related items found in the gas station building are from the family's collection.

Hundreds of tourists visit the Techatticup Mine each year. The Werly family provides historic mine tours, that take visitors into areas of the hard rock mine where they see the quartz veins that gold and silver ran in. The walking tour is approximately an hour and 20 minutes along a quarter-mile gravel path. Reservations are required for the tour.

With the backdrop of old cars, buildings and antiques the site is excellent for family photos, weddings, music videos, and movies.

Visit eldoradocanyonminetours.com for more information.

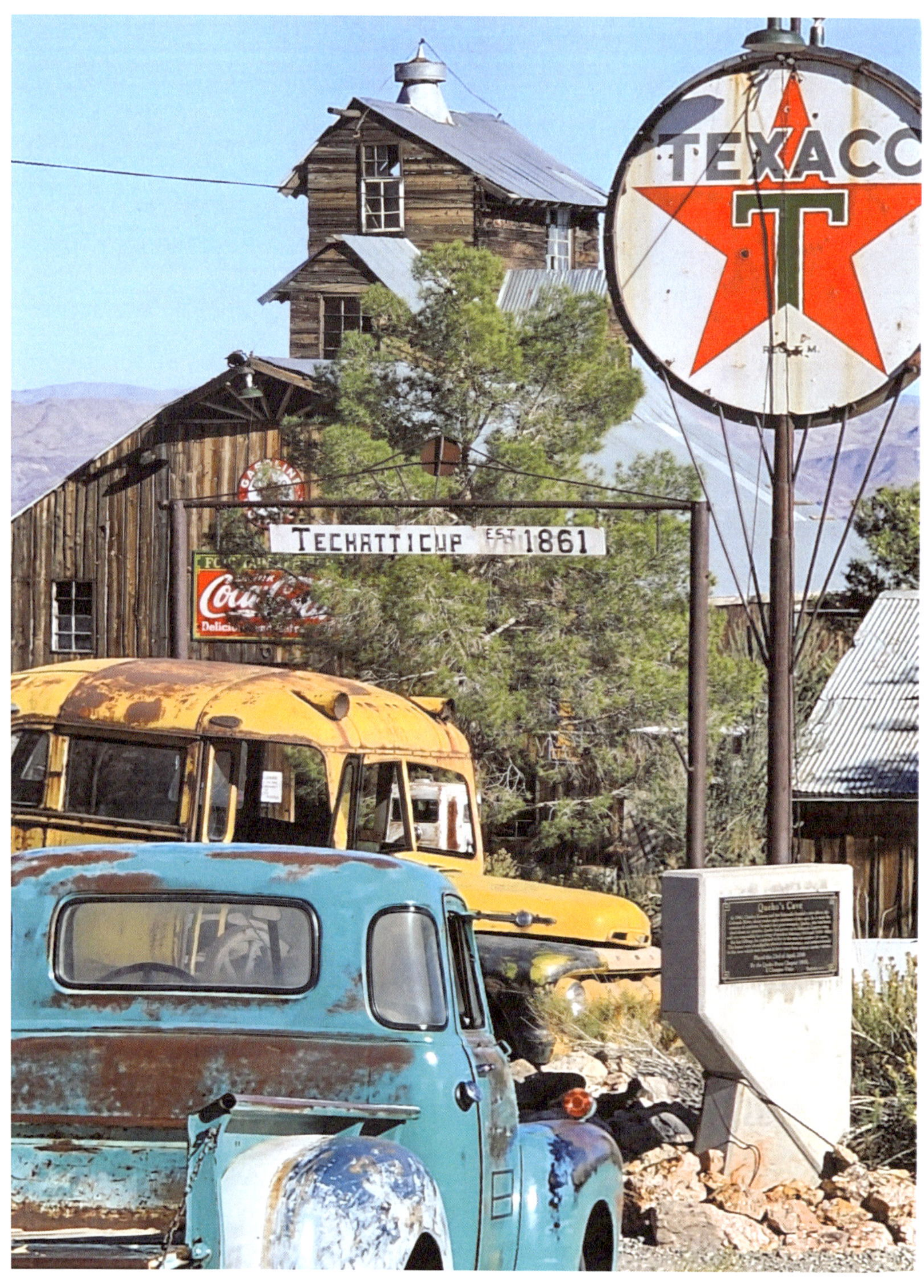

TEXACO
TECHATTICUP EST 1861
Coca-Cola

General Store

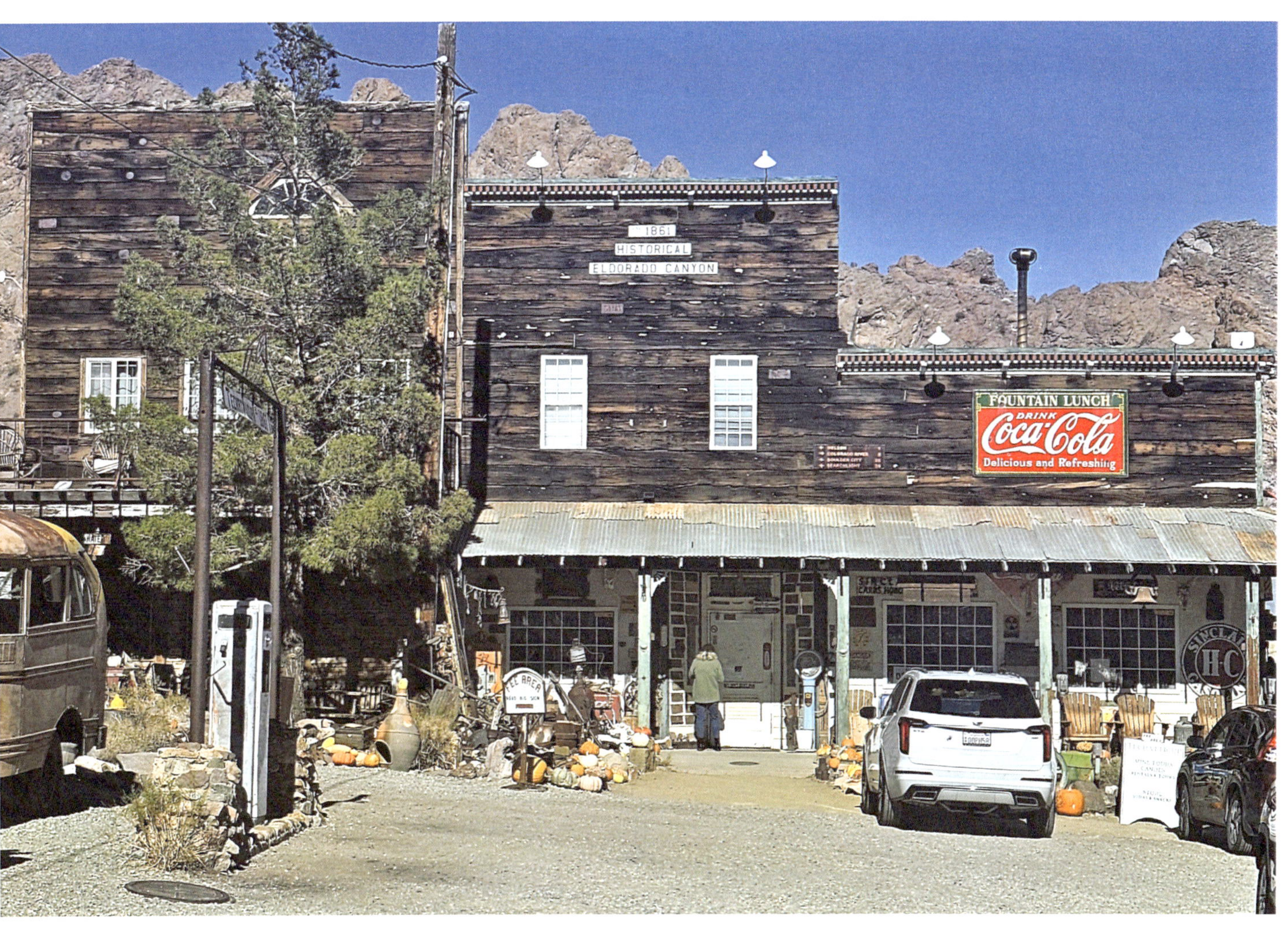

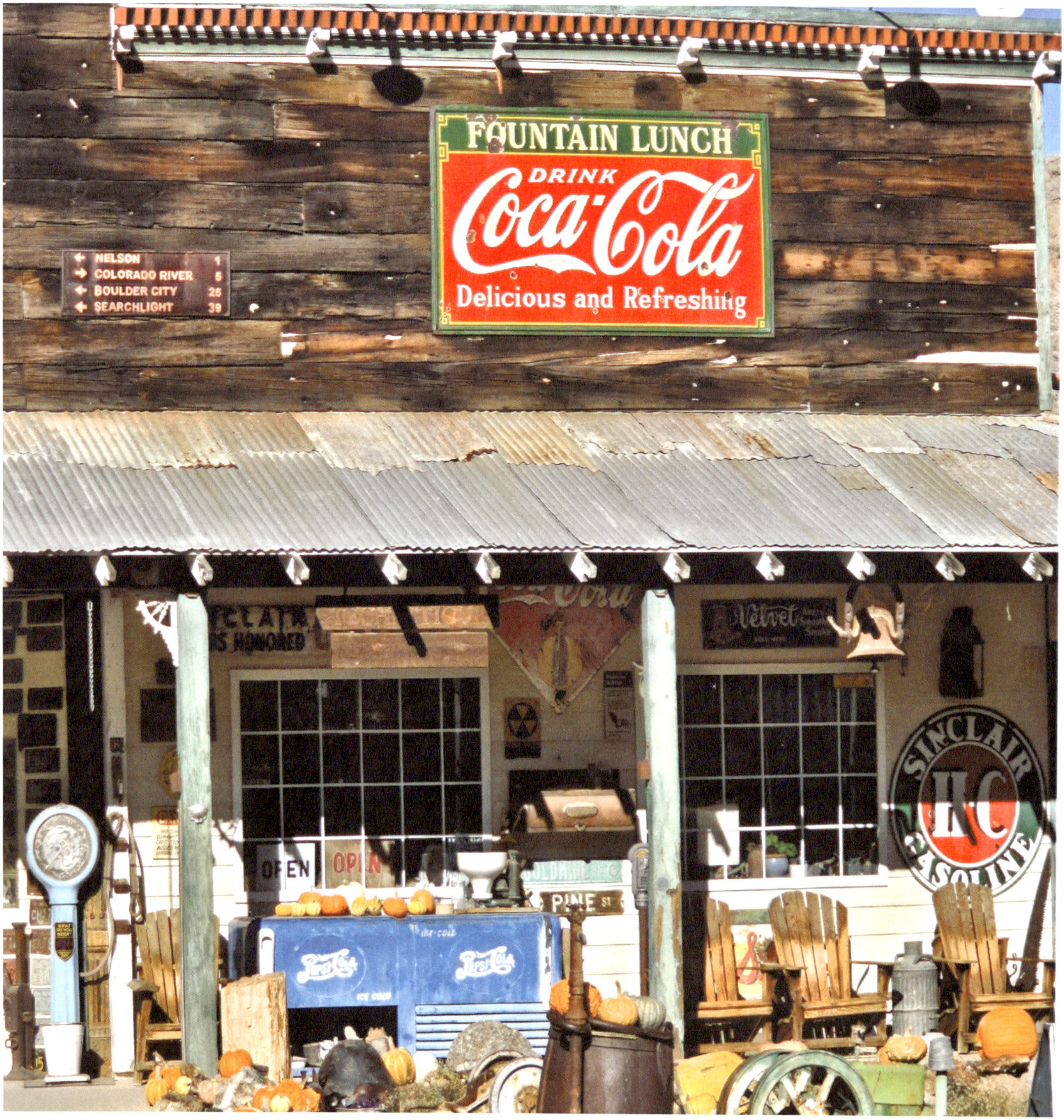

FOUNTAIN LUNCH
DRINK
Coca-Cola
Delicious and Refreshing
NELSON 1
COLORADO RIVER 5
BOULDER CITY 25
SEARCHLIGHT 39
Velvet
IS HONORED
OPEN
OPEN
PINE ST
Pepsi-Cola
Pepsi-Cola
ICE COLD
SINCLAIR
HC
GASOLINE

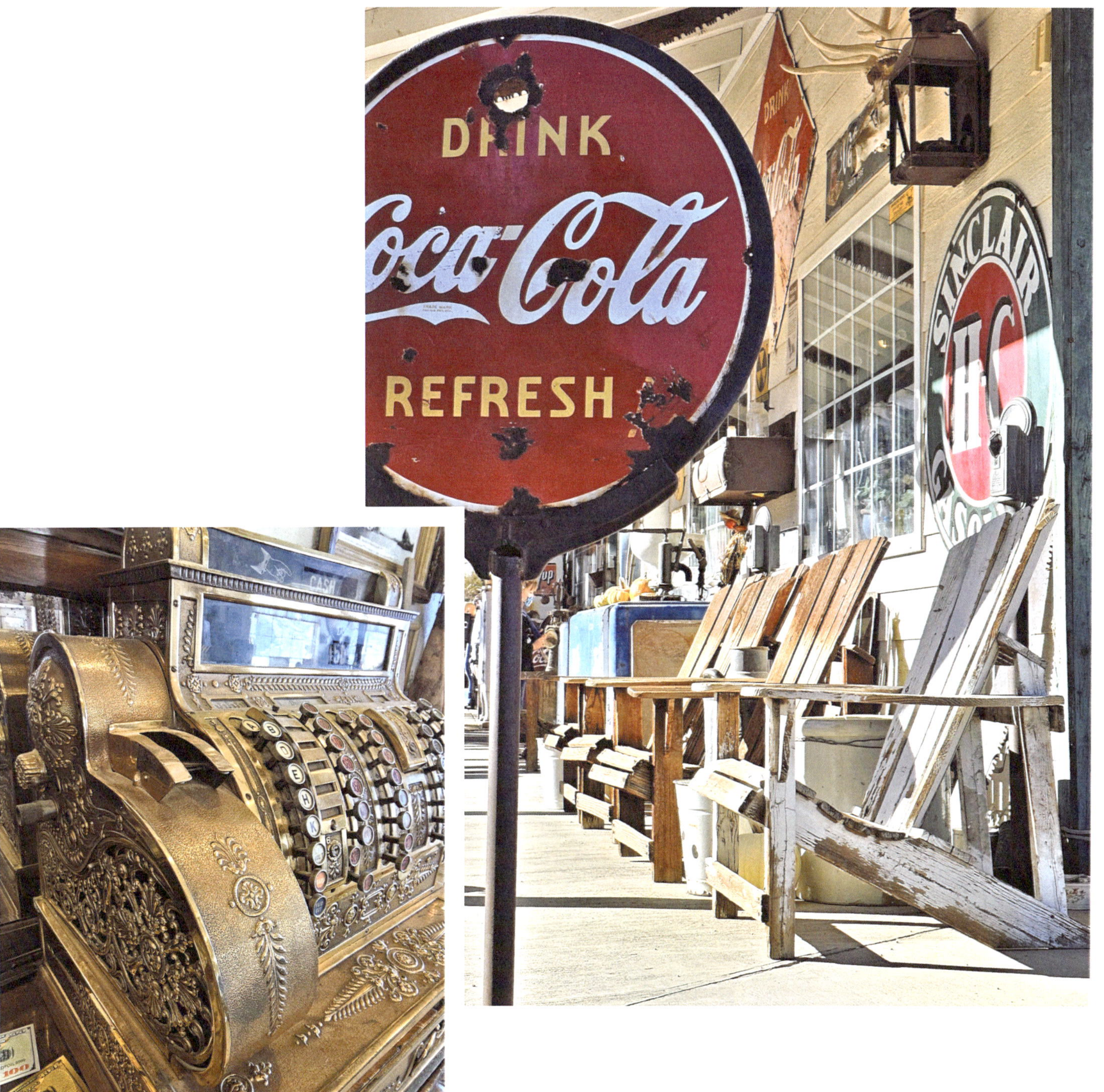
DRINK
Coca-Cola
REFRESH
DRINK
Coca-Cola
SINCLAIR
HC
CASH

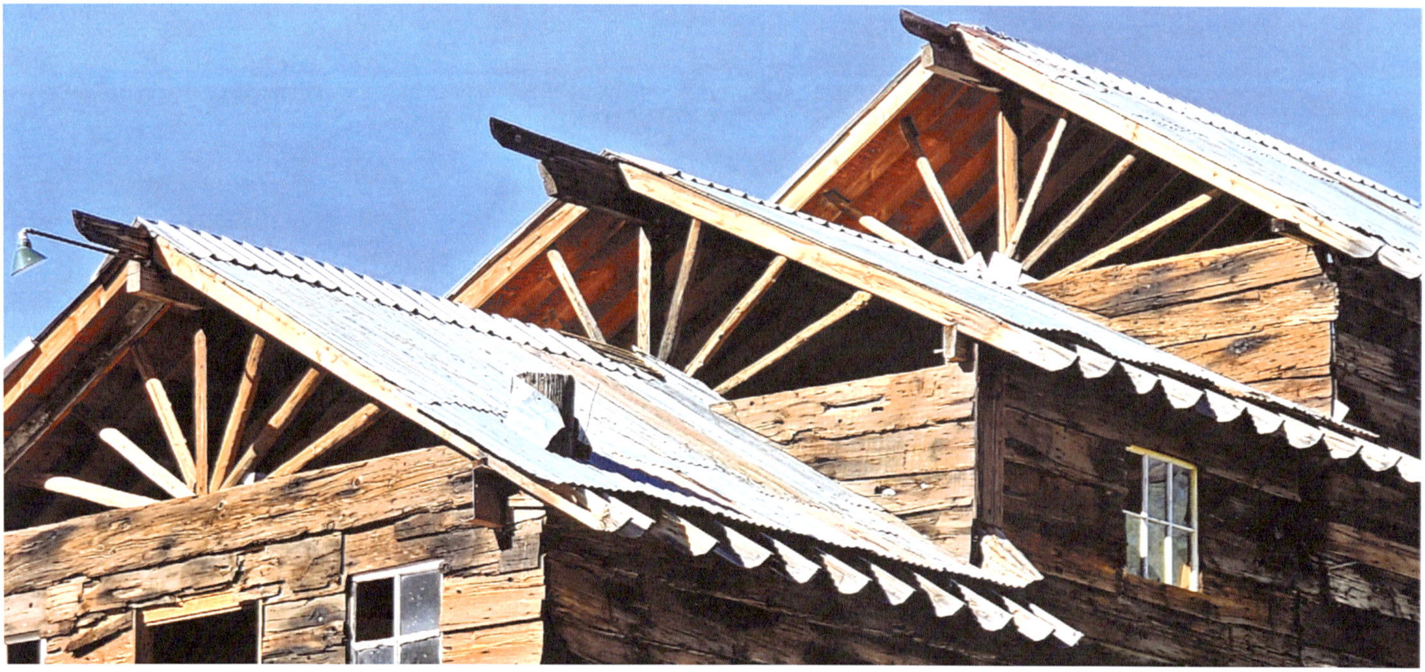

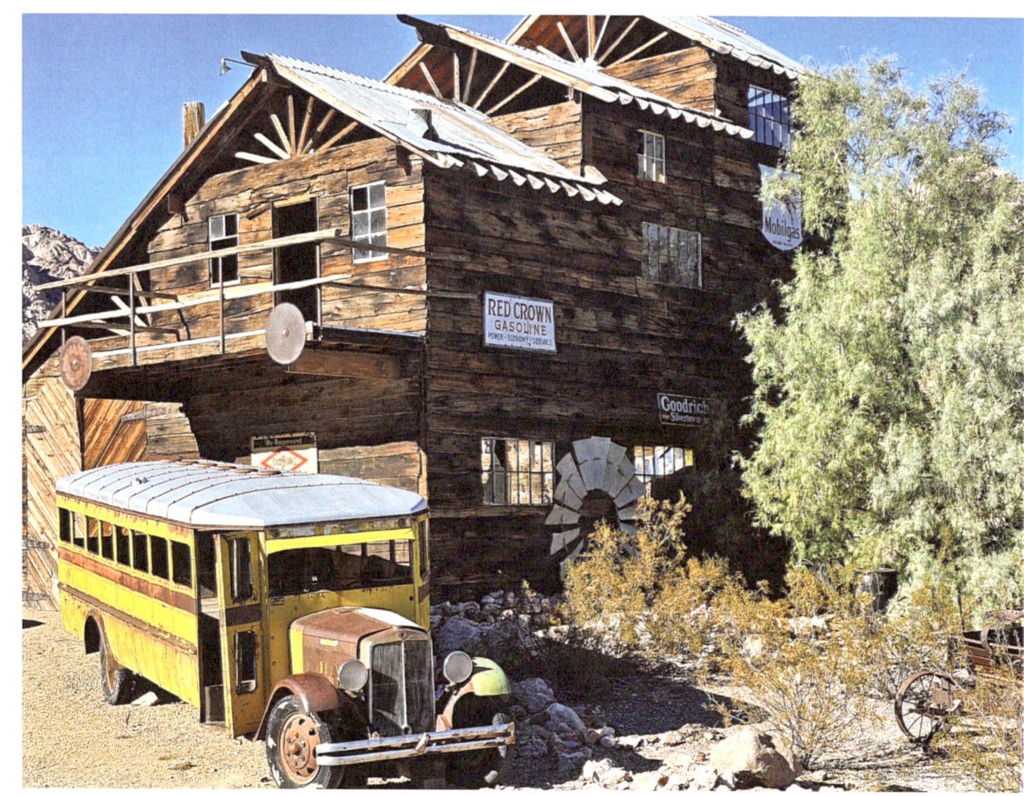
RED CROWN
GASOLINE
POWER · ECONOMY · SERVICE
Mobilgas
Goodrich

Restored Buildings

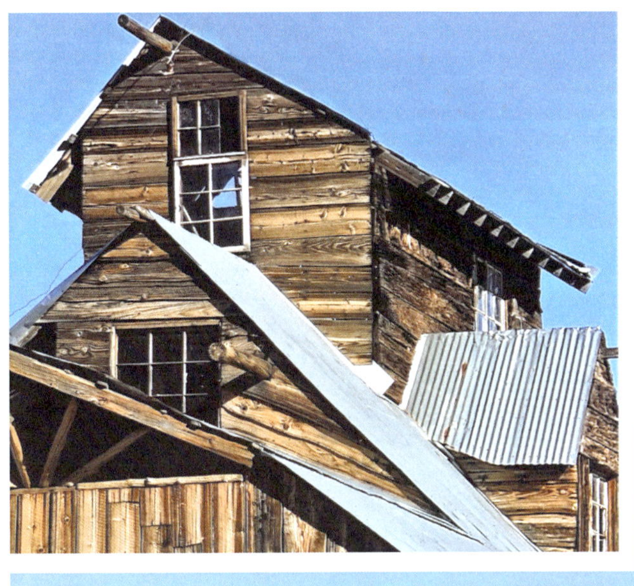

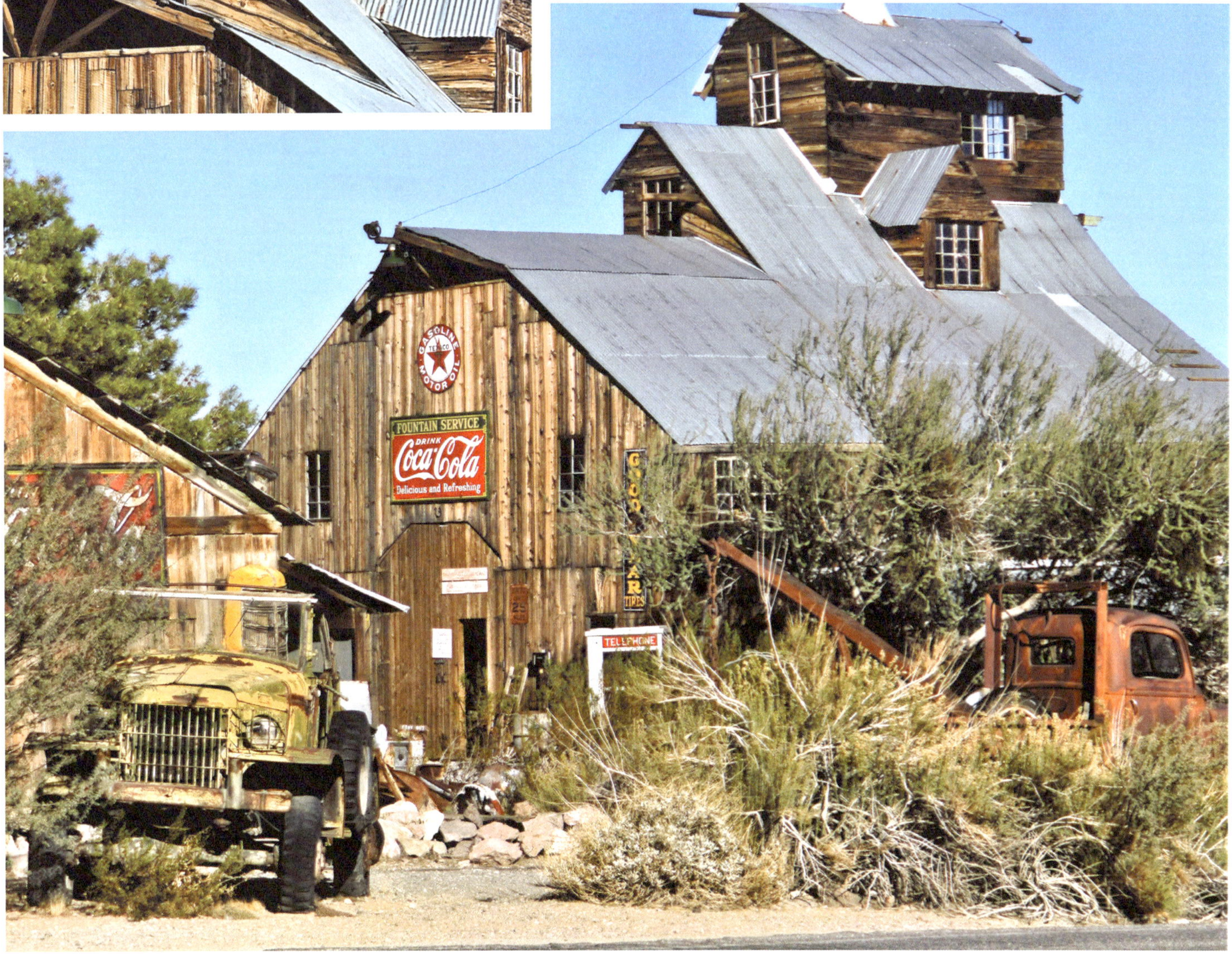

Open-air Church

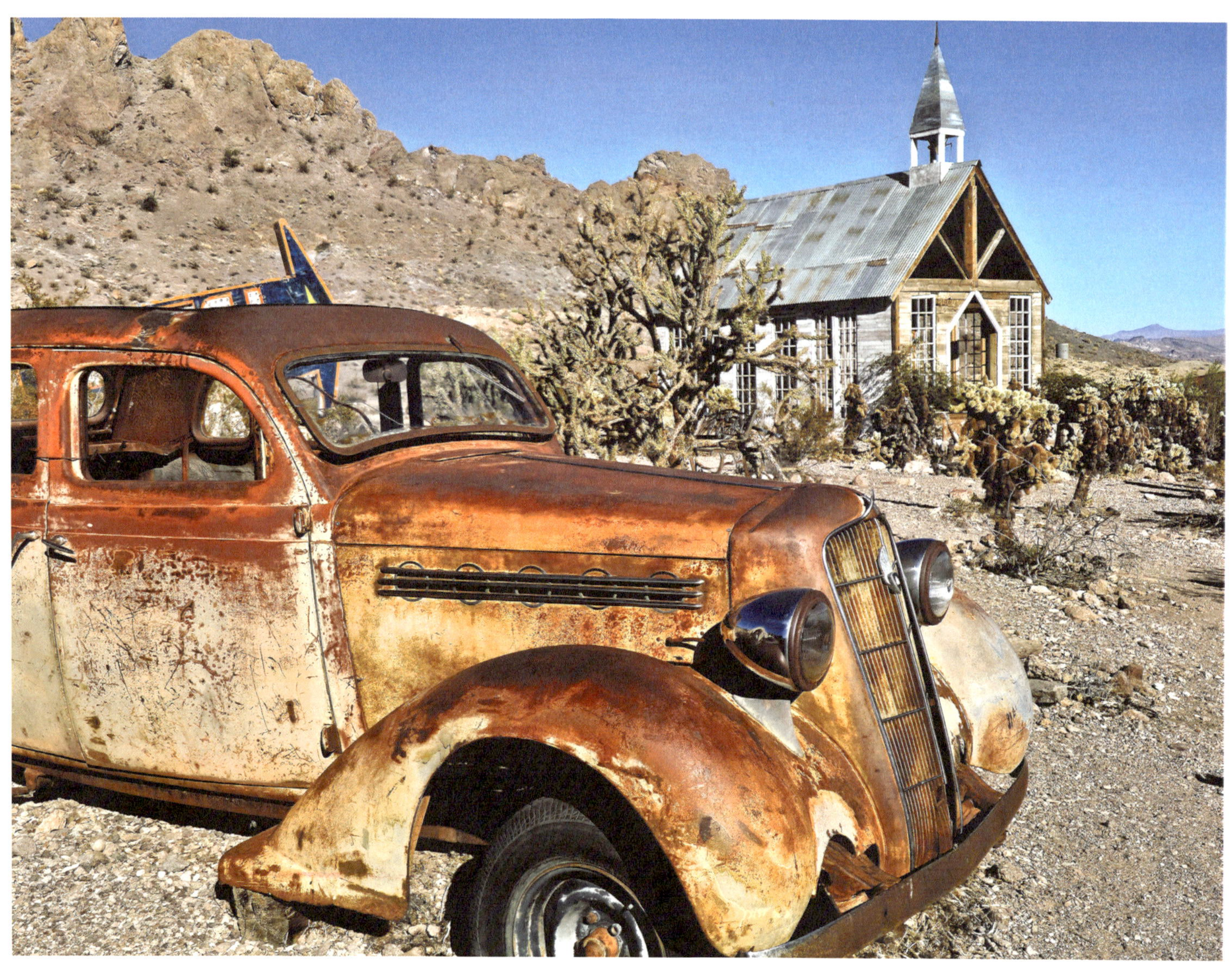

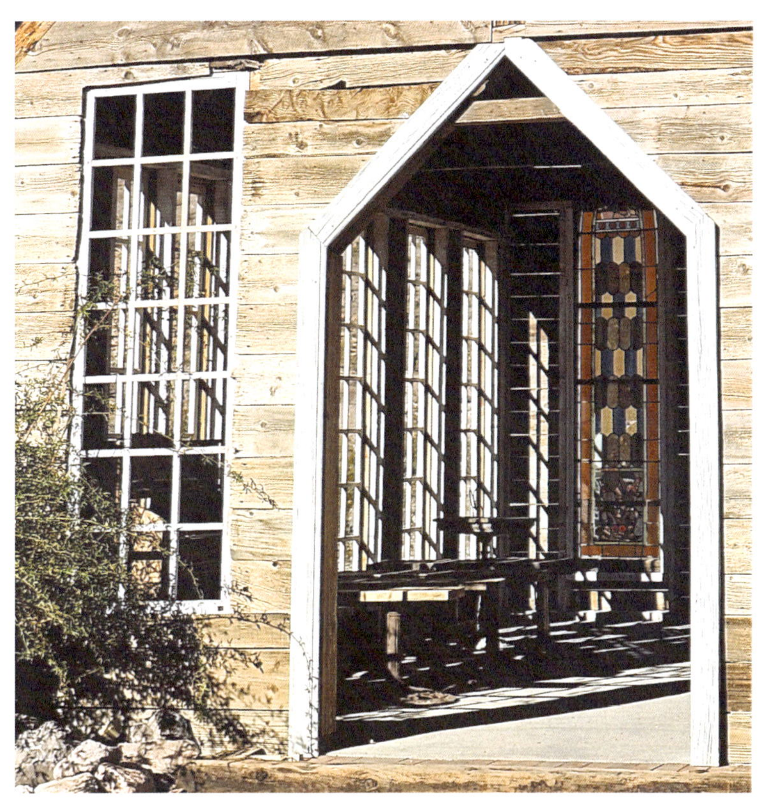

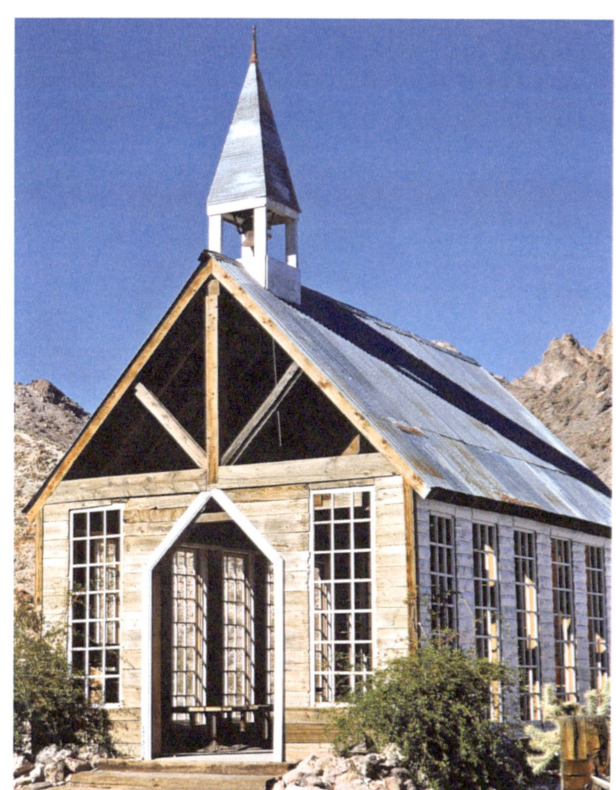

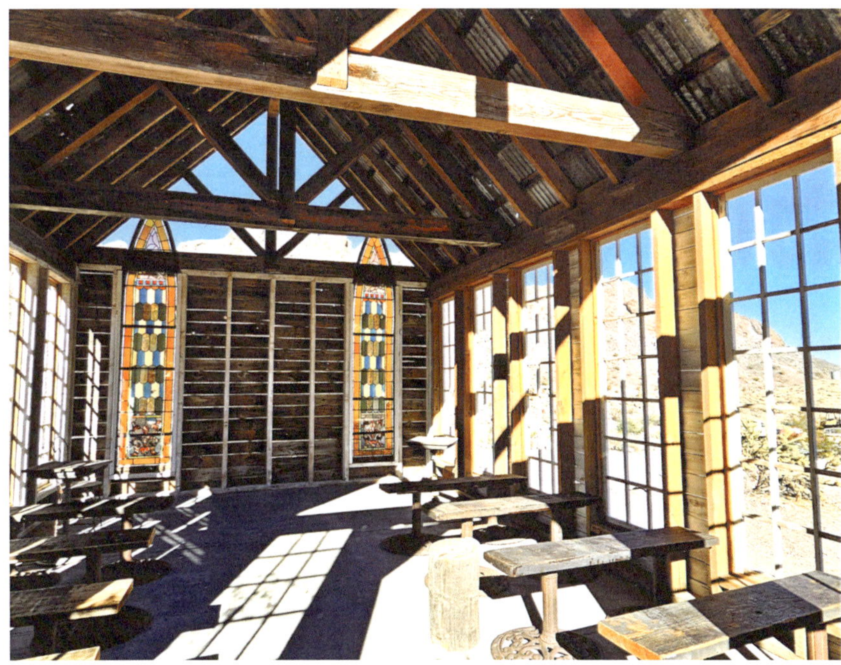

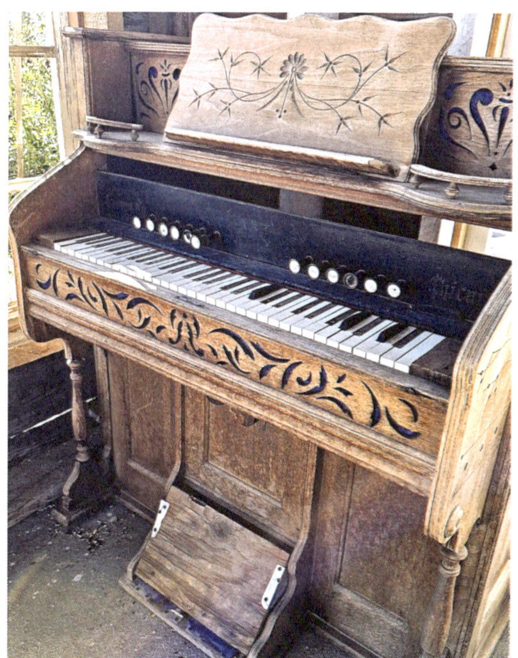

Gas Station

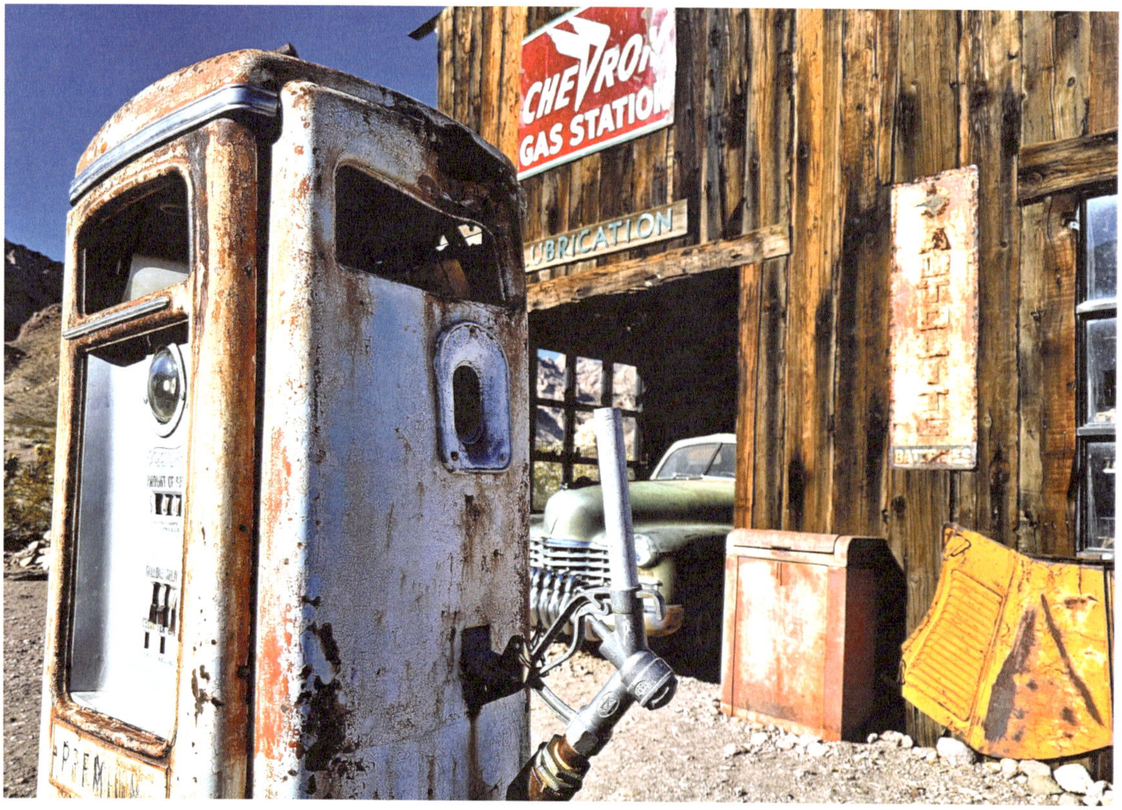

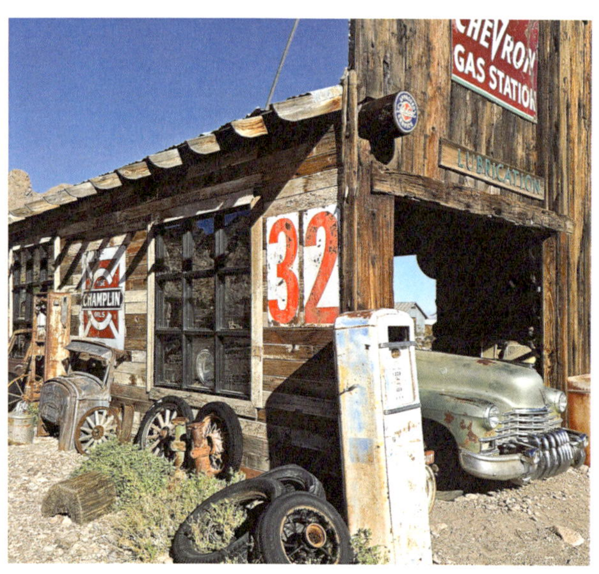

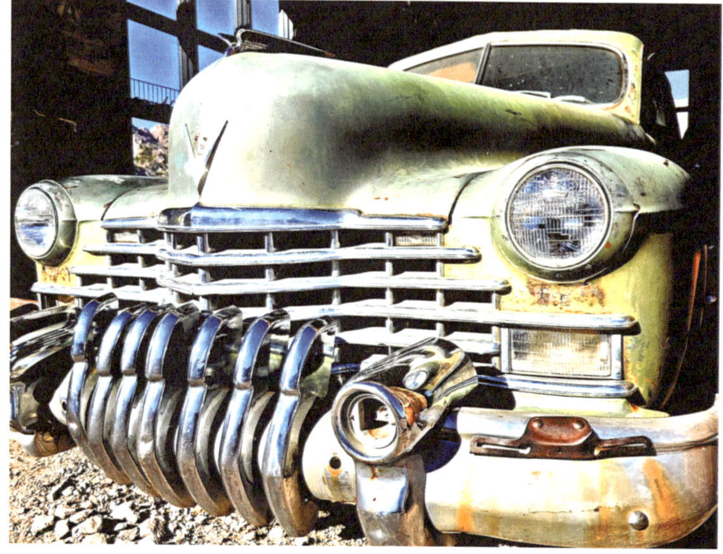

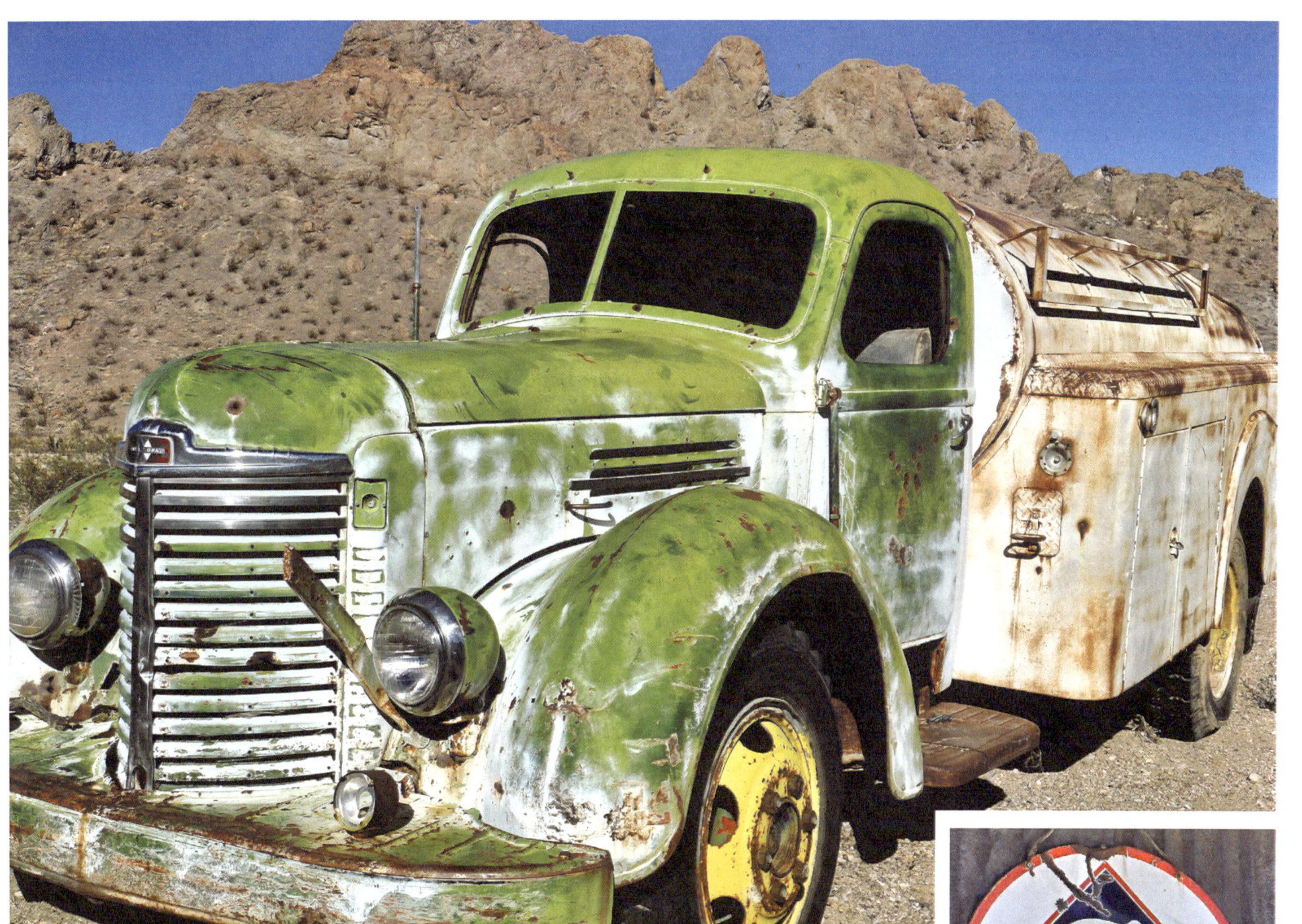

INTERNATIONAL
SKELLY
GASOLINE
Buy it Here

Water Tank and Tanker Truck

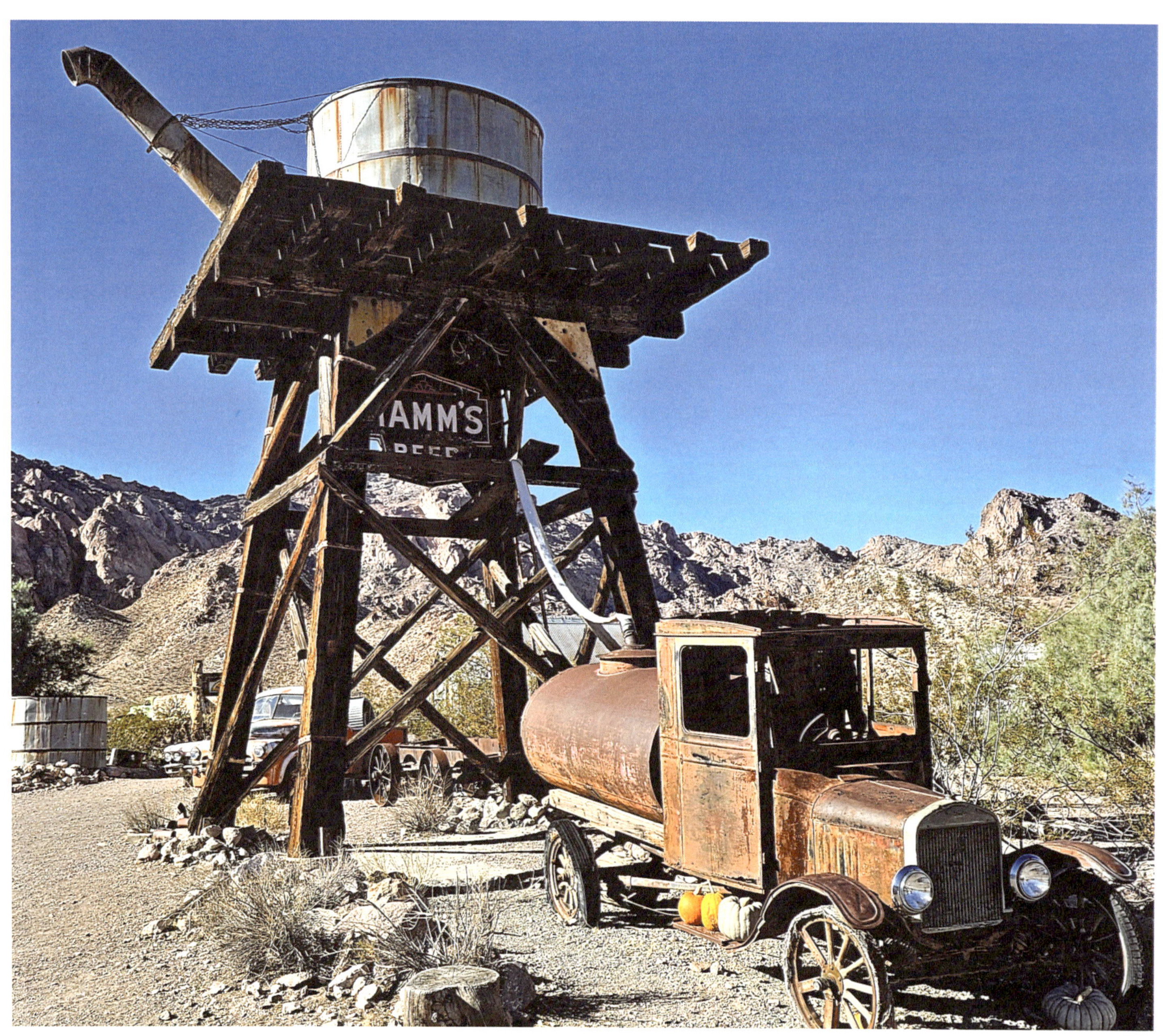

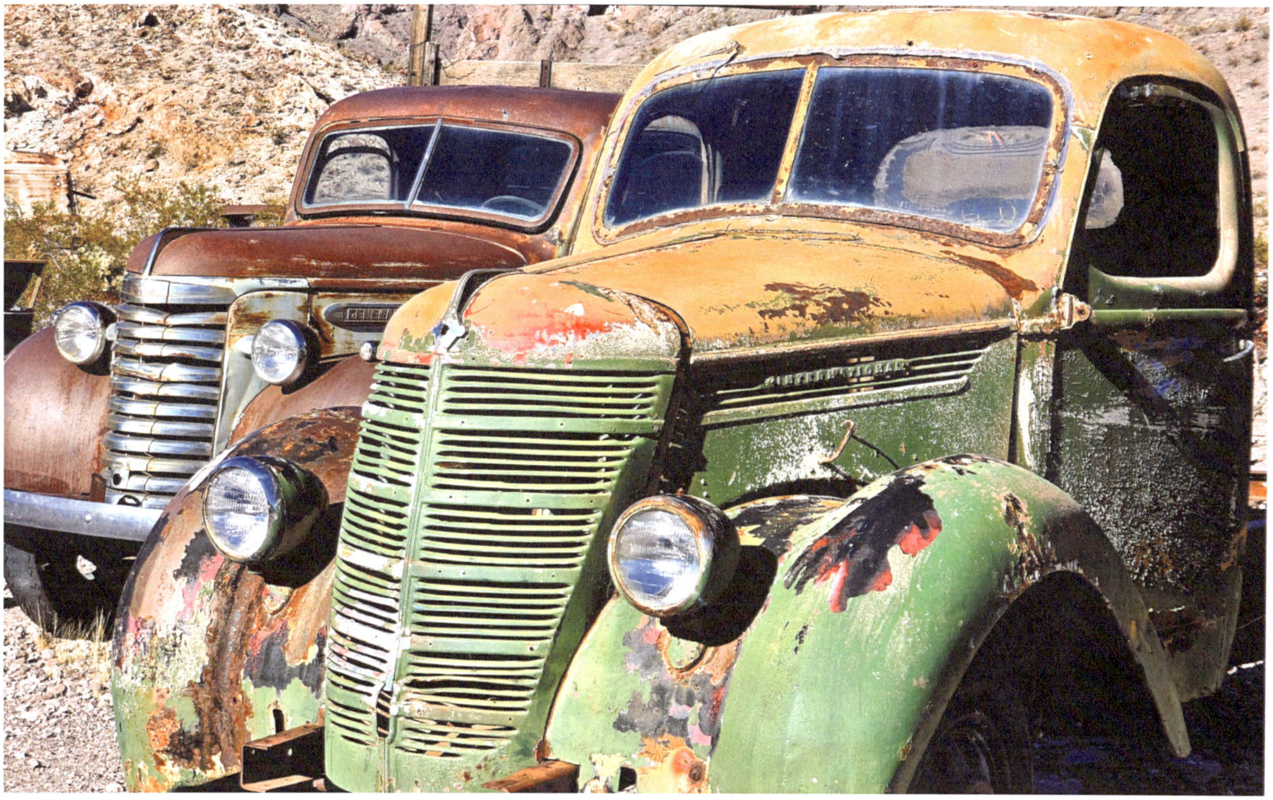

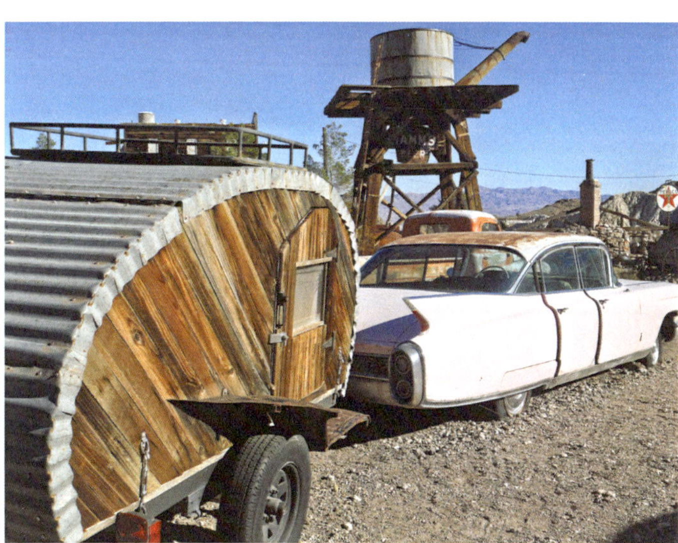

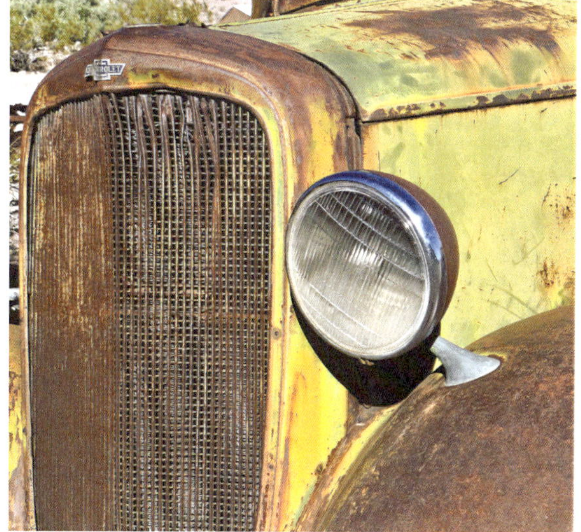

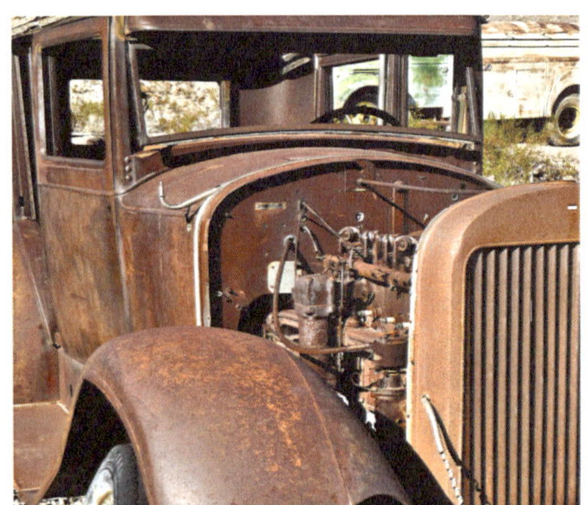

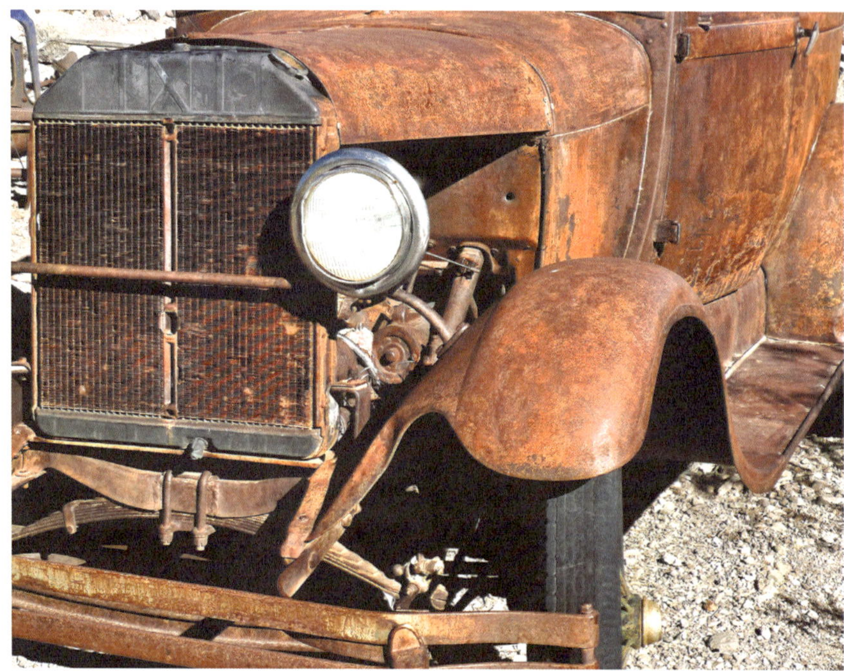

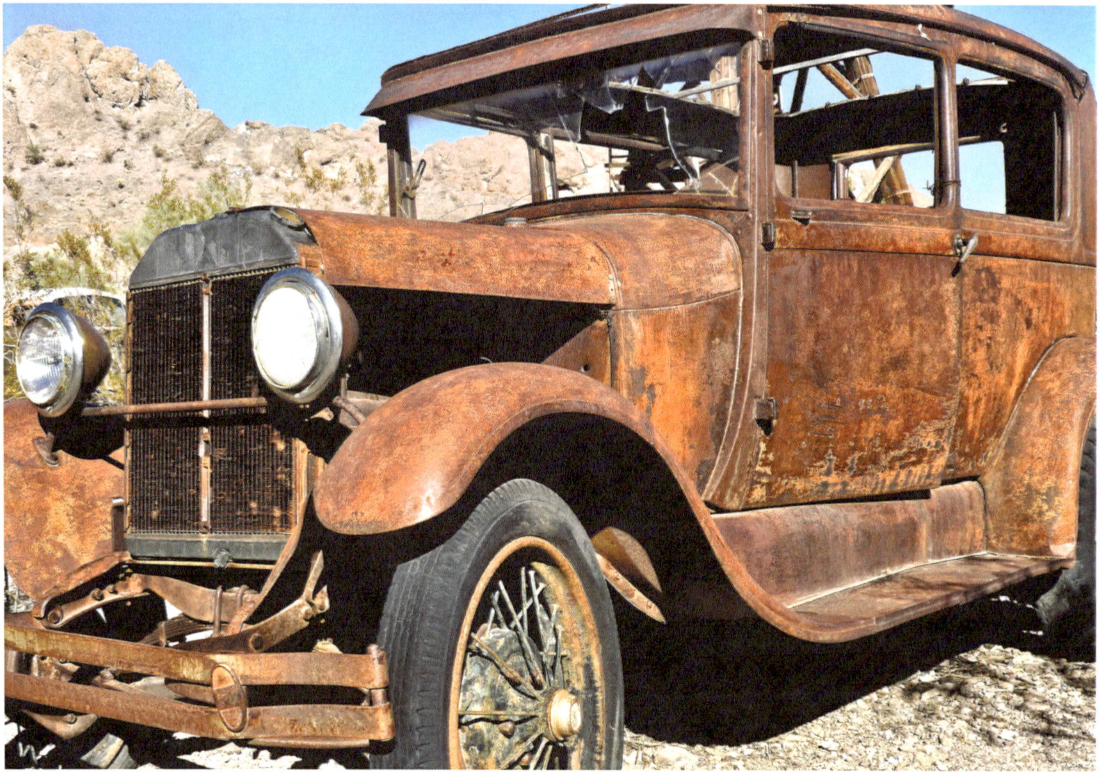

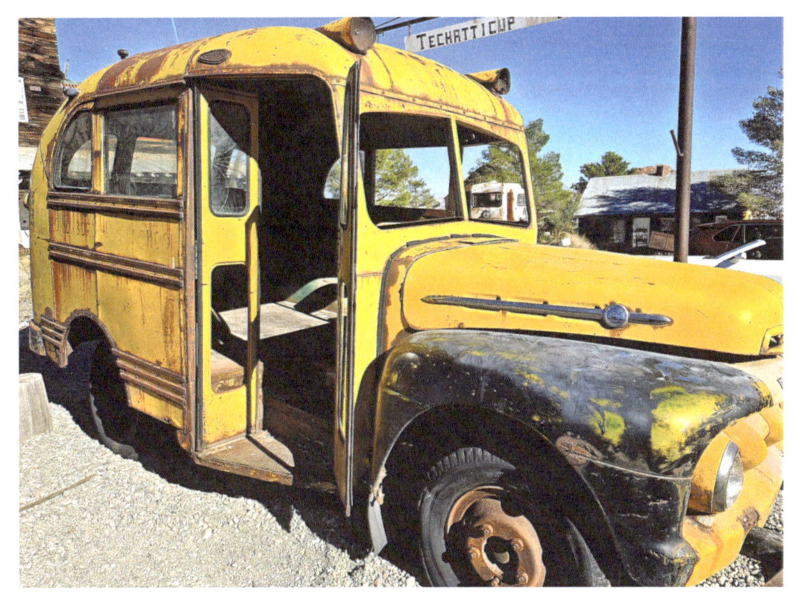

School Buses

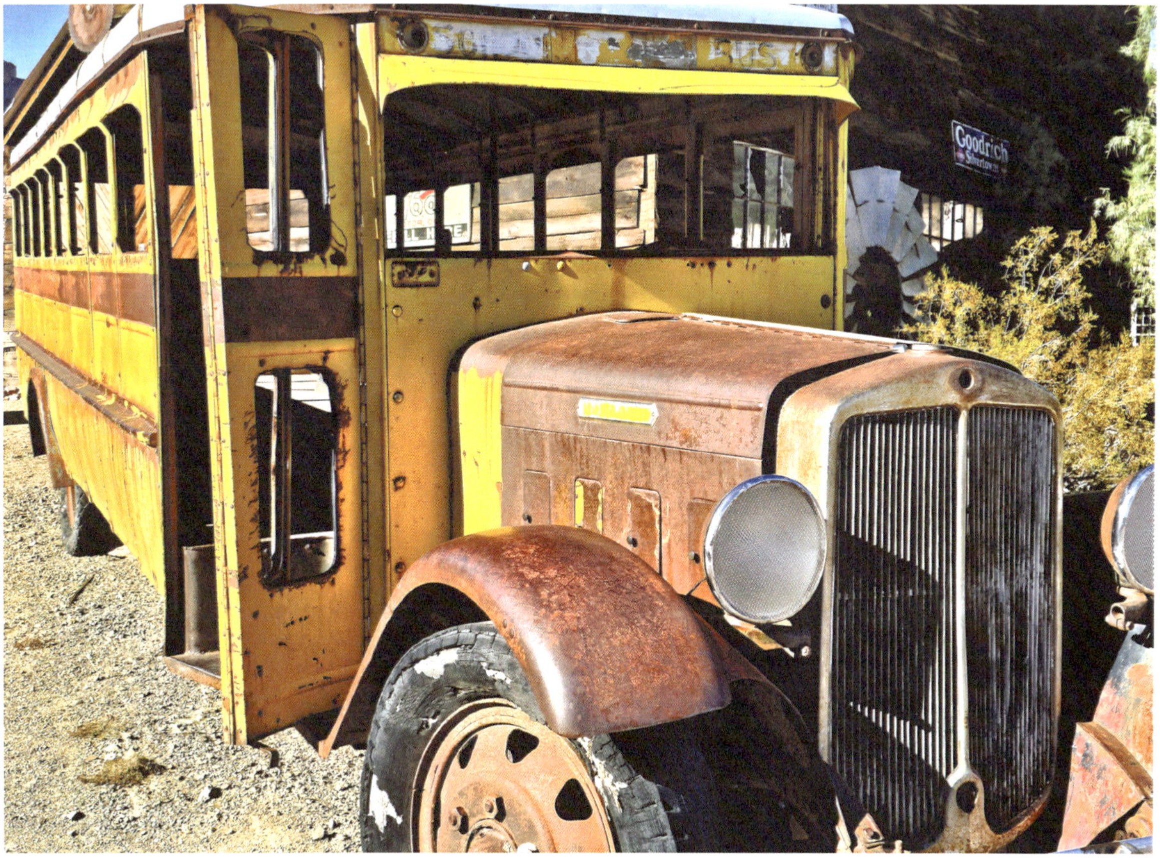

Signs of the Times

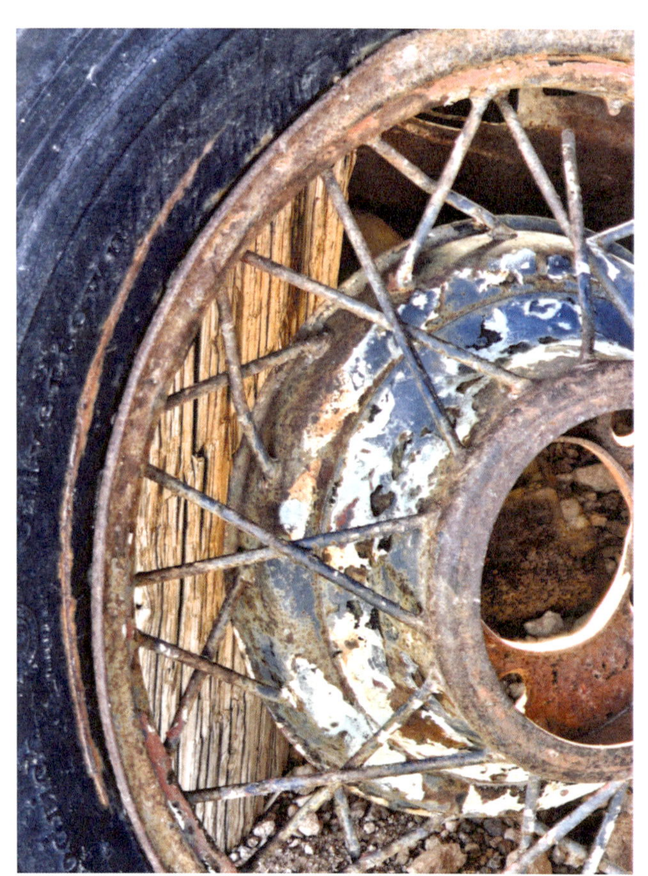

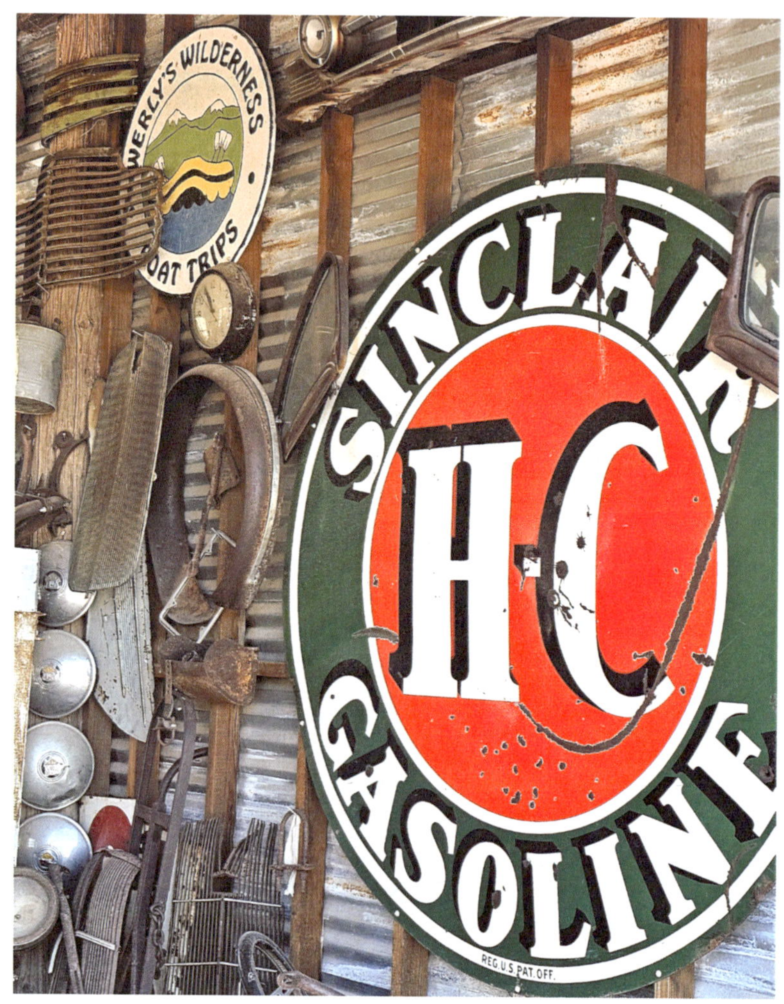

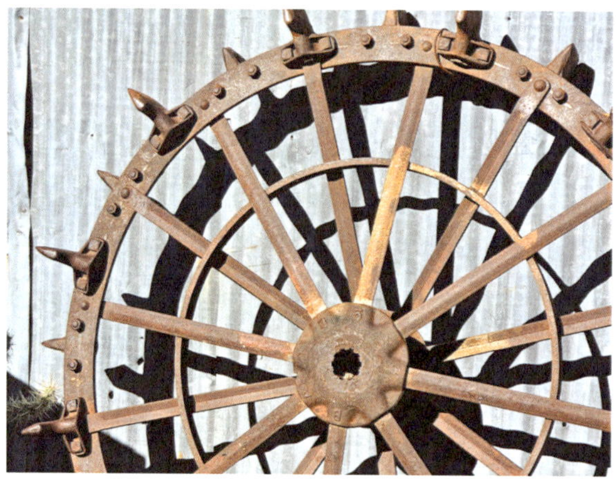

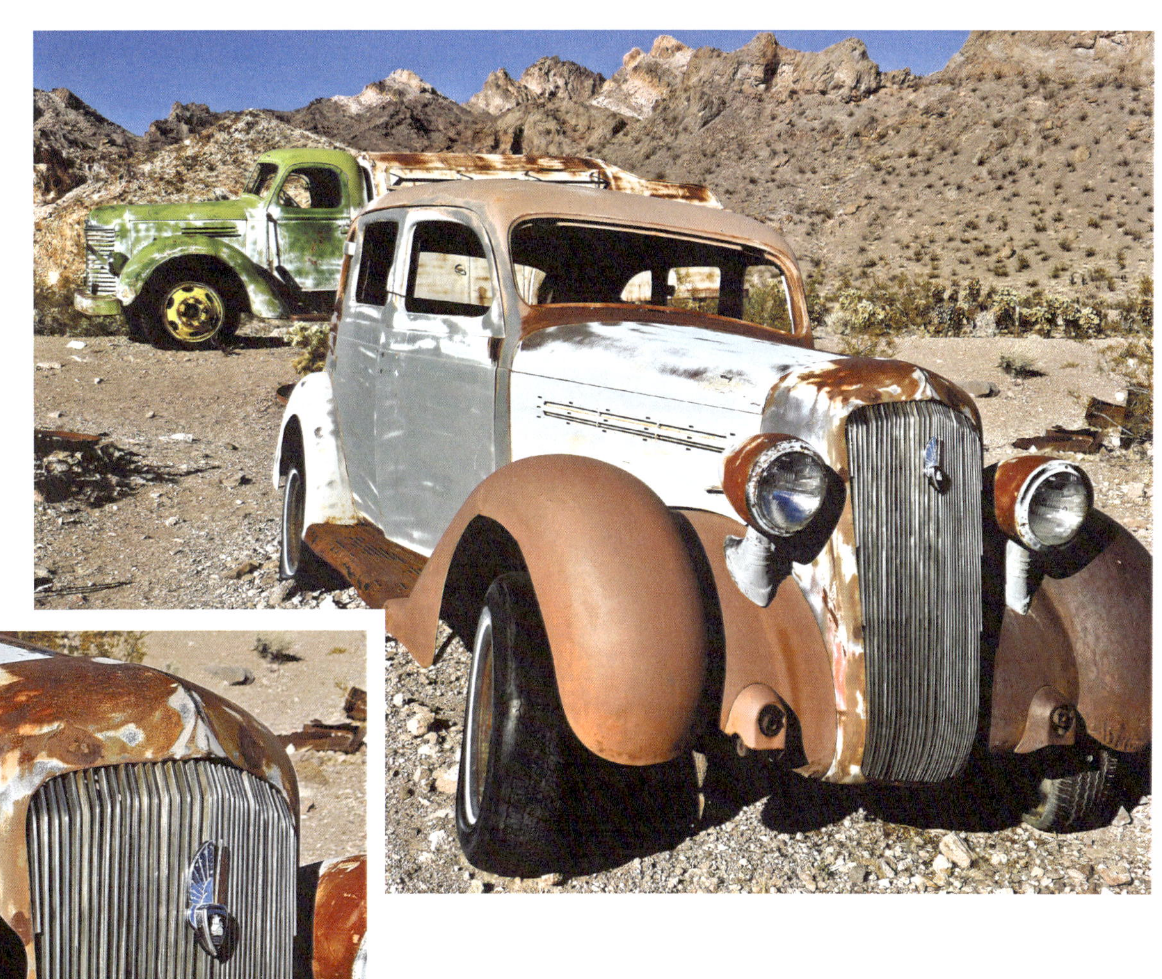

Cabin Remains

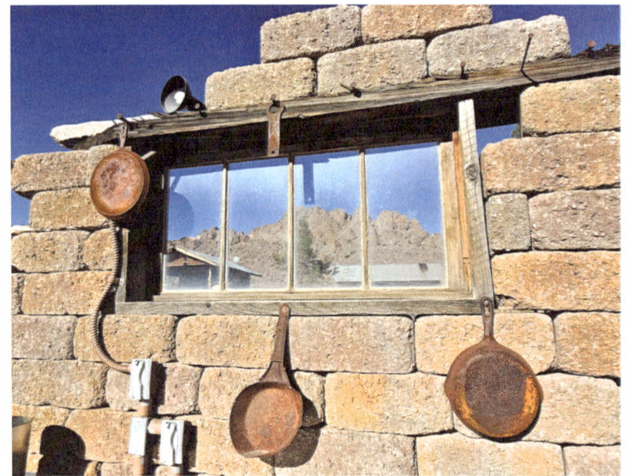

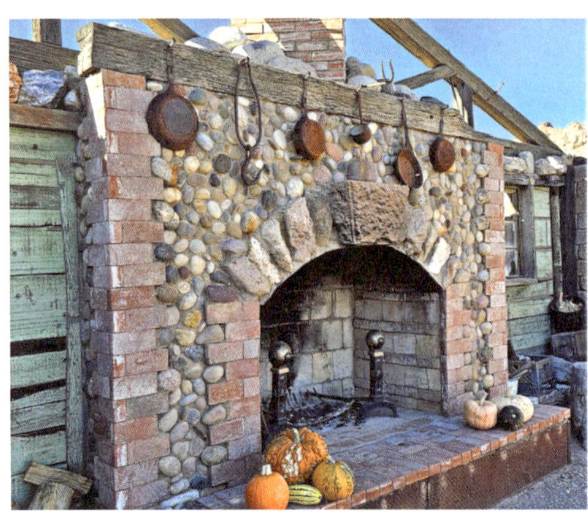

All that remains from one cabin is the fireplace and part of two walls.

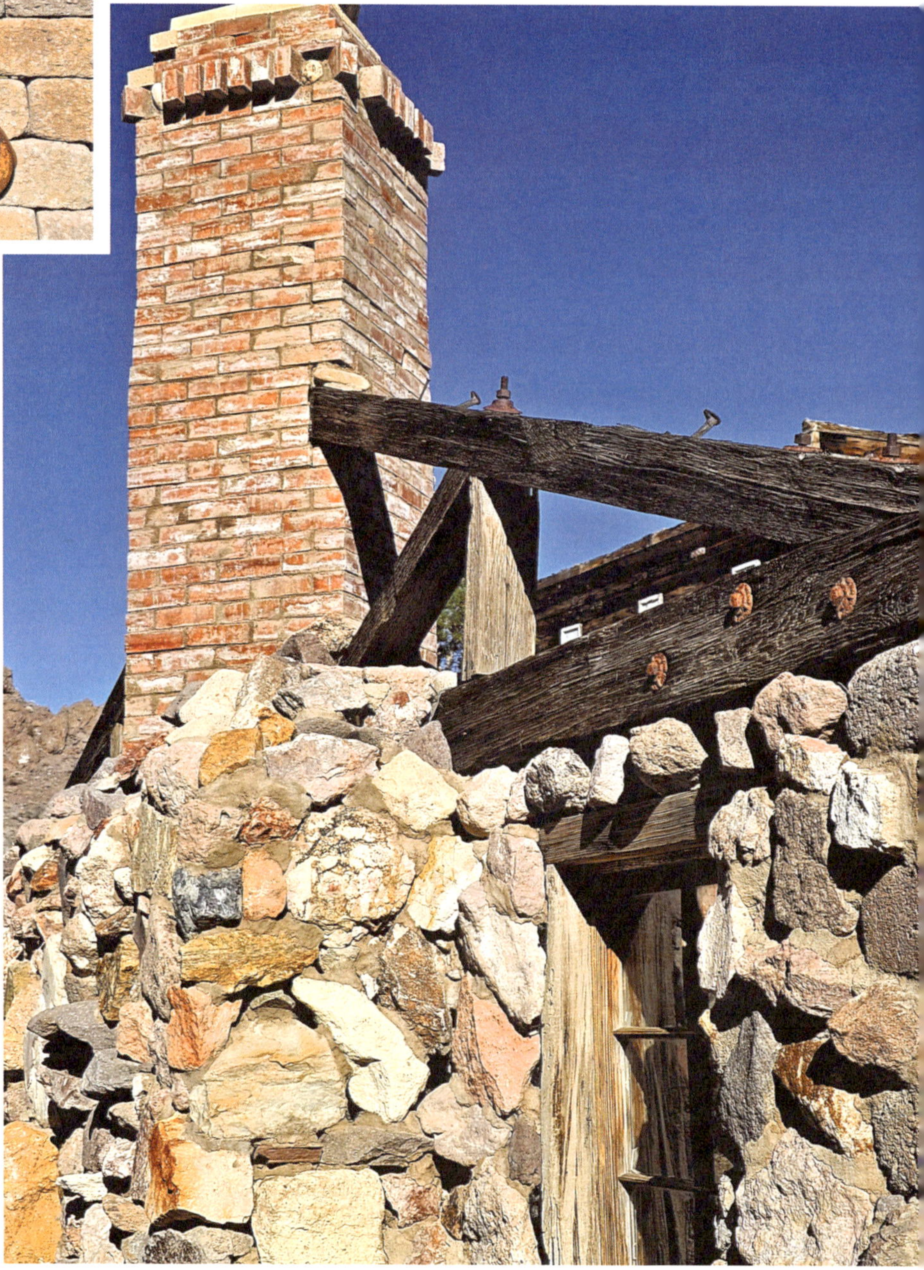

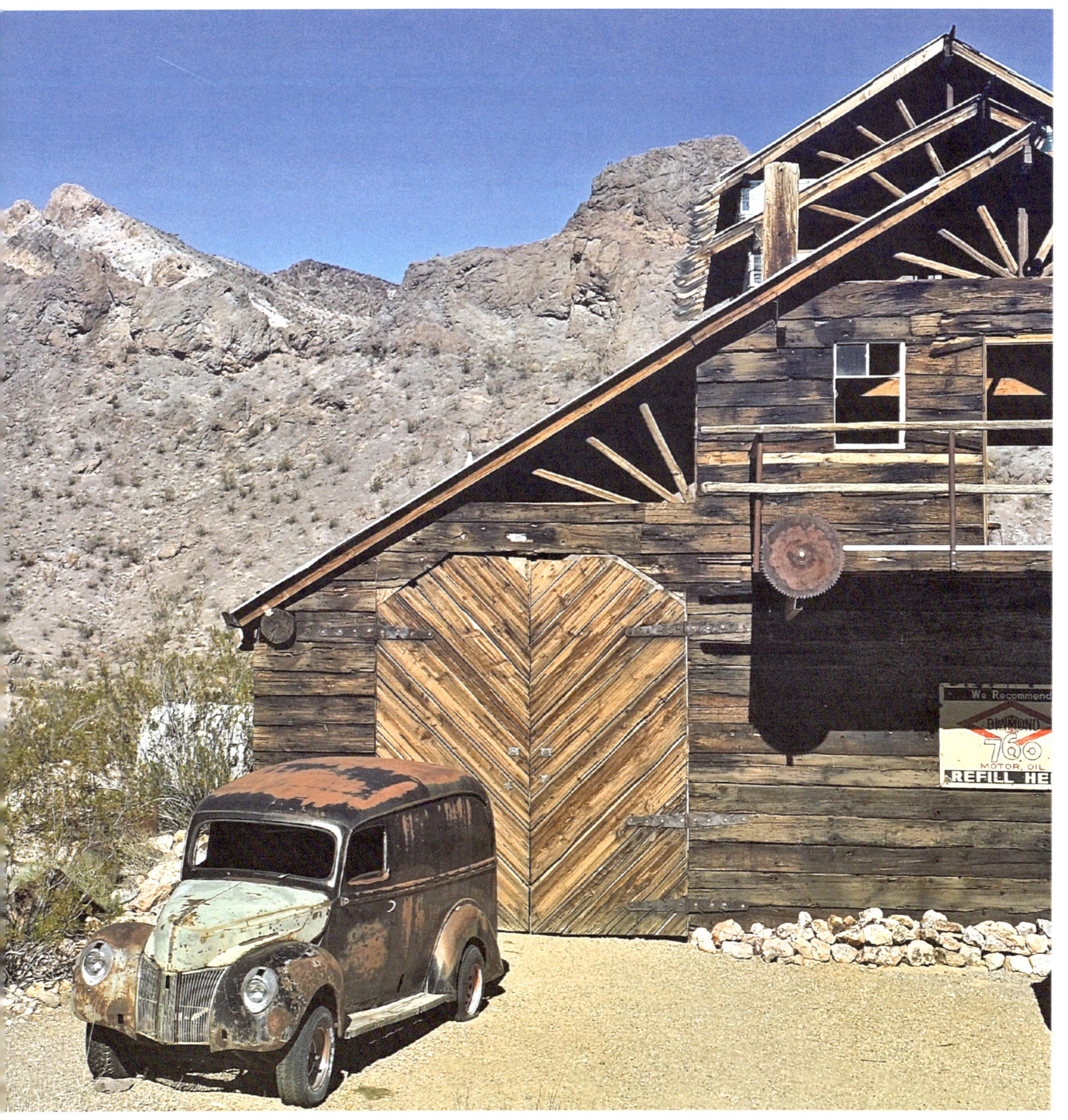
We Recommend
DIAMOND
760
MOTOR OIL
REFILL HE

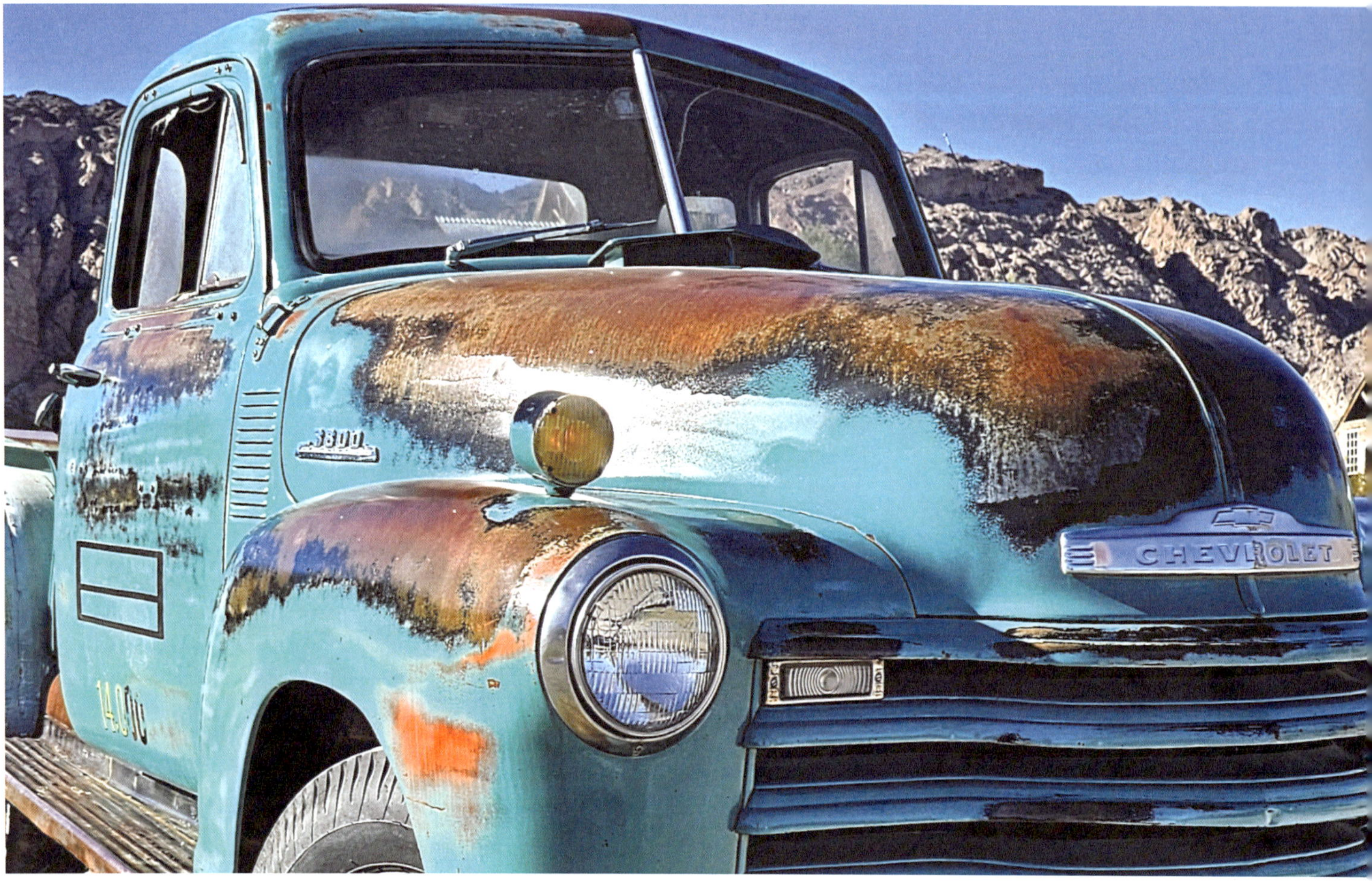

About the Photographer

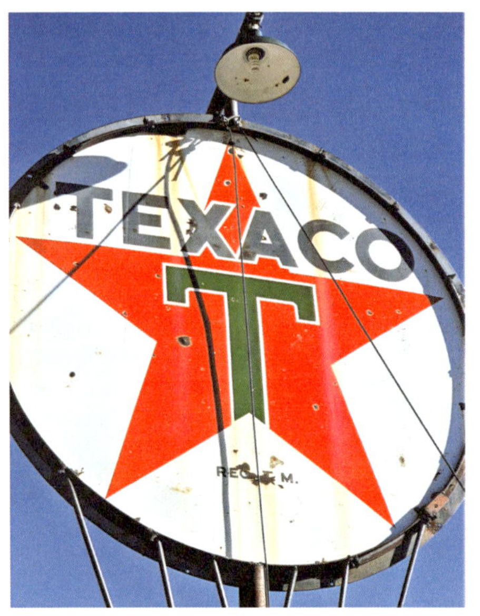

Jane Moorman describes herself as an adventurer who loves to drive backroads to see what there is to see.

During her 30-year journalism career, Jane honed her photograpic skills as a photojournalist including covering high school sporting events.

A friend once said, "I wish I could see the world as Jane sees it. Finding the beauty in things that most of us don't take time to see."

Upon retiring in 2021, Jane decided there is a lot of her native country she had not visited, so she began her journey of exploring the USA.

She currently lives in Albuquerque, New Mexico, but says her real home is on the road.